The Christmas Penny

By Ian N LoCurto

Illustrations by Susan Anderson Shorter

AuthorHouse™
1663 Liberty Drive
Bloomington, IN 47403
www.authorhouse.com
Phone: 1-800-839-8640

© 2010 Ian N LoCurto. All rights reserved.

No part of this book may be reproduced, stored in a retrieval system, or transmitted by any means without the written permission of the author.

First published by AuthorHouse 7/1/2010

ISBN: 978-1-4490-7100-4 (sc)

Library of Congress Control Number: 2010909291

Printed in the United States of America
Bloomington, Indiana

This book is printed on acid-free paper.

I dedicate this book to my family. Thank you for being my ears when I couldn't hear, my light when times were dark, and my strength when I was weak. I love you all so very much.

It was a cold and snowy night the time this story came to be. You see, there once was an old man who lived in a city much like our own. One night, after his cocoa mug was empty and the fire had settled down, he decided to go for a walk by himself to take in the sights and smells of winter in the city. This man was not a wealthy man, nor was he famous, but what happened that Christmas Eve night made him the wealthiest and most famous man who ever lived.

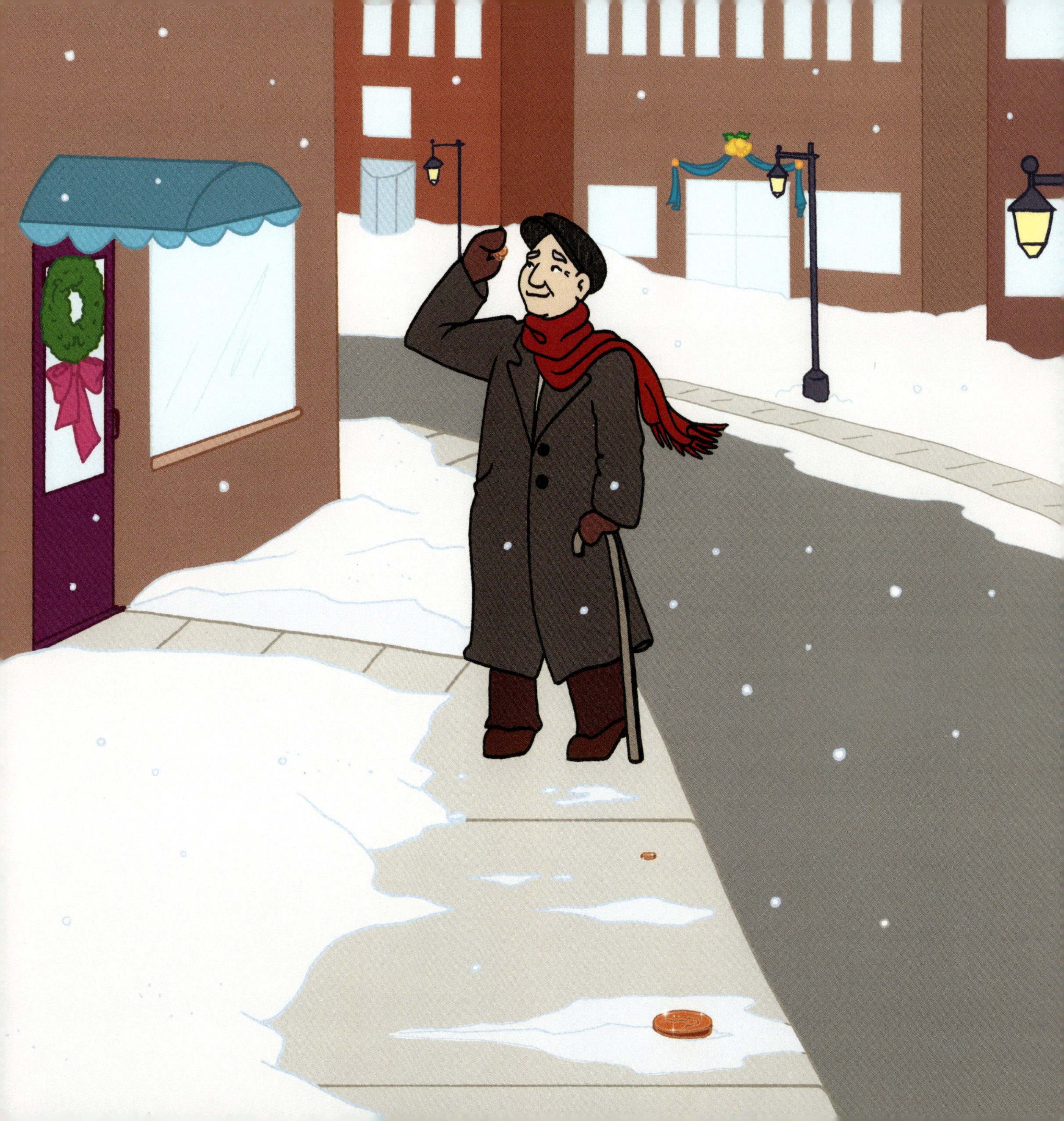

As the snow crunched beneath his feet and his cane tapped the long lost pavement beneath, he noticed, every so often, pennies lying in the street—unwanted pennies that people had gotten rid of because of sheer fact that pennies in society today can't really buy you anything, unless saved up. Every unwanted penny he saw, he picked up, wiped off, and placed into his pocket. He realized after wiping them all off that every one of them was different. Each one told its own story.

Some were younger, cleaner, and shinier than the others. Some were older, dirtier, and had been around much longer. No matter how you looked at it, they were all pennies.

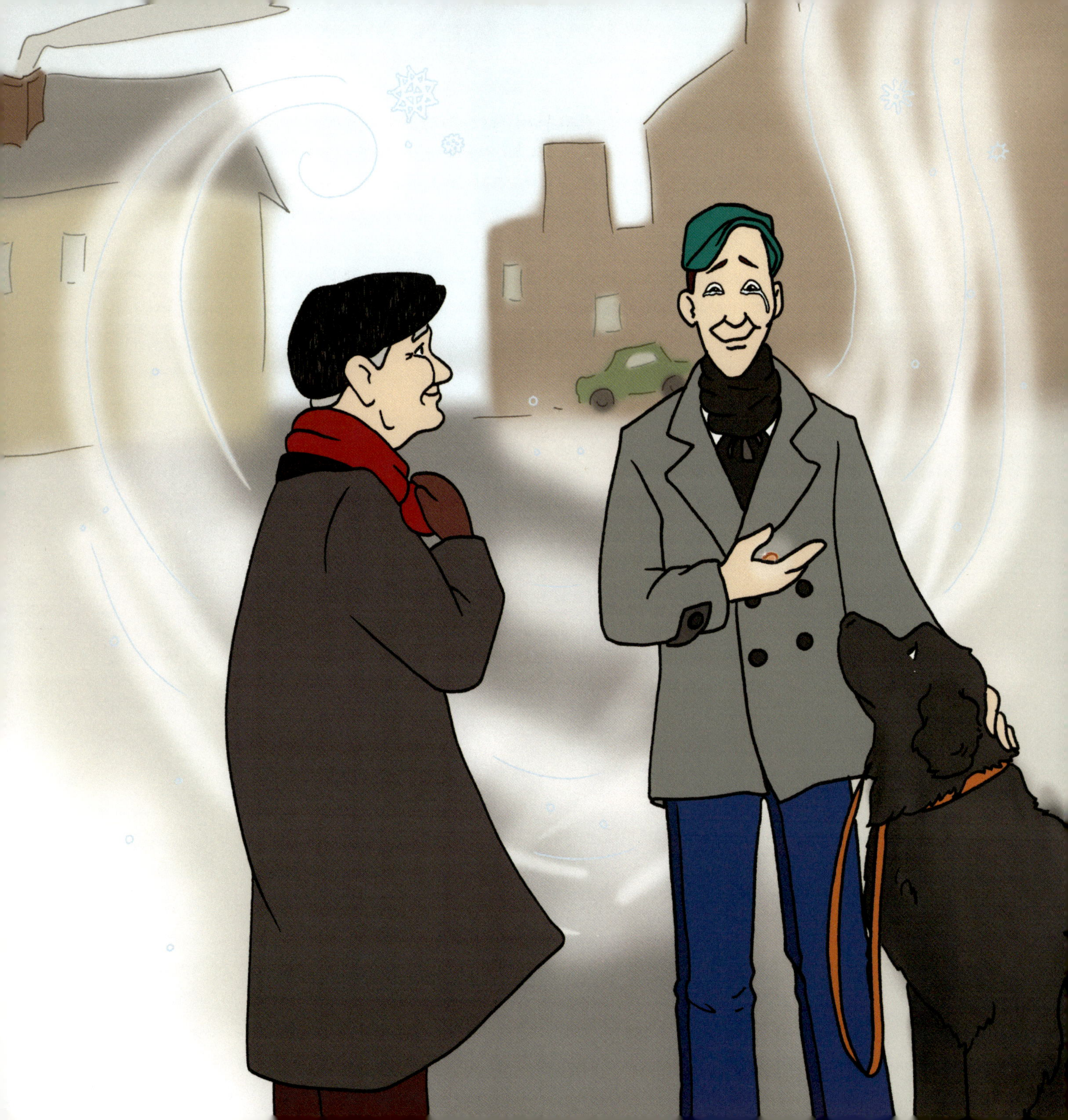

While walking, he came across a much younger man who was walking his dog. The man's head was low; he did not look like he knew Christmas was the next day. They both greeted each other with a Merry Christmas, and as the distance between them grew further, the old man stopped and turned around. "Sir," he said.

"Yes," replied the gentleman.

"I do not mean to pry, but it seems as though your Christmas spirit is lost. I was never really the type of person who was good at cheering people up or doing spontaneous things, but might I ask you a silly question?"

"Okay," said the gentleman.

"What year were you born?"

Astonished, he looked up and boldly spoke up and said, "Nineteen seventy-nine."

"Very good," said the older man. At that moment the older man began searching through his unwanted pennies. Penny after penny he searched, and in amazement he looked down and saw the year 1979. He looked at the gentleman and said, "I do not have much to give, and I do not know what to say to make your problem go away, but if you take this penny and hold it close to your heart and make a wish, maybe, just maybe, things will begin to look brighter.

A lonely tear began to fall down the gentleman's face. The older man looked at him and said "Sir, are you all right?"

The man glanced his way and said, "I do not know why I am telling you this, but it just seems right. A year ago my father passed away. At his bedside he told me that he would always be with me. I asked him, "Father, how will I know? He told me that one day I would meet an elderly man whom I did not know. And this man would give me an unwanted penny from the year that I was born for no reason at all. 'It is with this act that you will know that I will always be with you,' he said. So sir, you see, over the last year I have felt that my father was never with me. But tonight, on this Christmas Eve, I know that he will always be here no matter what. Thank you, kind sir, for now I know.

The older man shed a tear and said, "You're welcome. Merry Christmas." And the gentleman disappeared as he walked away in the heavy snow.

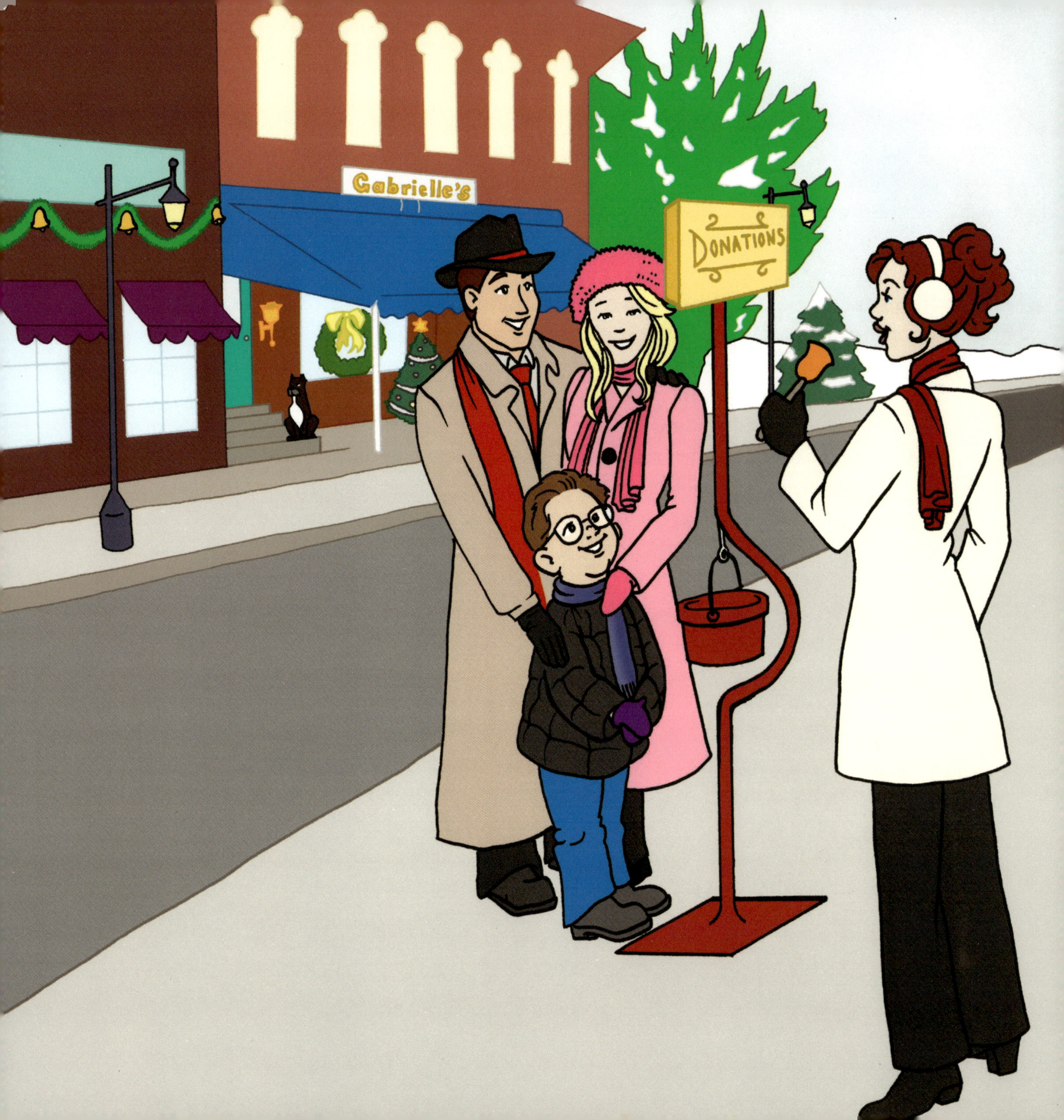
Gabrielle's
DONATIONS

The old man limped on in the snow, picking up every penny he saw. While walking, he noticed a figure in the distance. Because of the falling snow, he could not make out who it was, but the sound of the bell gave it away. As he limped on, taking in deep breaths of the beautiful winter night that it was, he looked up and saw who was standing there. A woman who had the smile of an angel stood there ringing a bell for a good cause. He also noticed from a distance a mother, father, and child standing in front of the lady.

"Go ahead, son; put your penny in the pot."

The boy reached into his pocket and started crying. "What's wrong, son?" the father asked.

The little boy looked up at his father and said, "Dad, it was here a minute ago, it must have fallen out of my pocket."

The older man saw this from a distance and approached the family. "Merry Christmas," he said.

"Merry Christmas" they said back simultaneously.

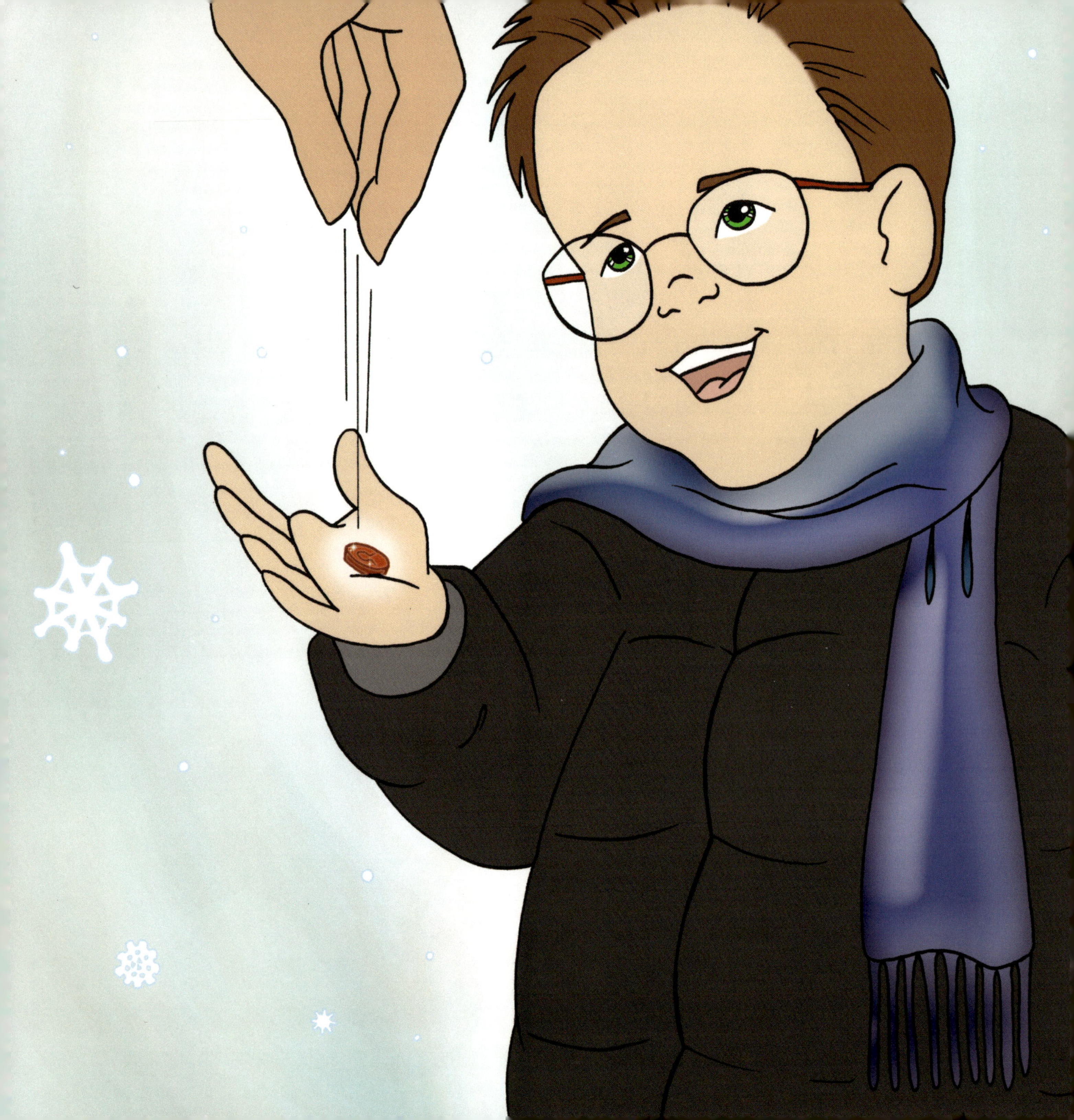

The old man reached into his pocket and placed a penny in the child's hand. "Close your eyes and make a wish, and maybe, just maybe, your wish will come true."

The boy looked at the penny, closed his eyes, and made a wish. He placed the penny in the pot. "Thank you, sir," the boy replied.

"Might I ask what you wished for?" said the man.

The little boy looked up and said, "I wished that the penny I put into the pot would multiply so that every little boy and girl could never go hungry again."

A smile came from all of their faces. The older man looked and said, "I do too, young man.

"Merry Christmas," he said to all of them. He then placed some money in the pot himself and limped on.

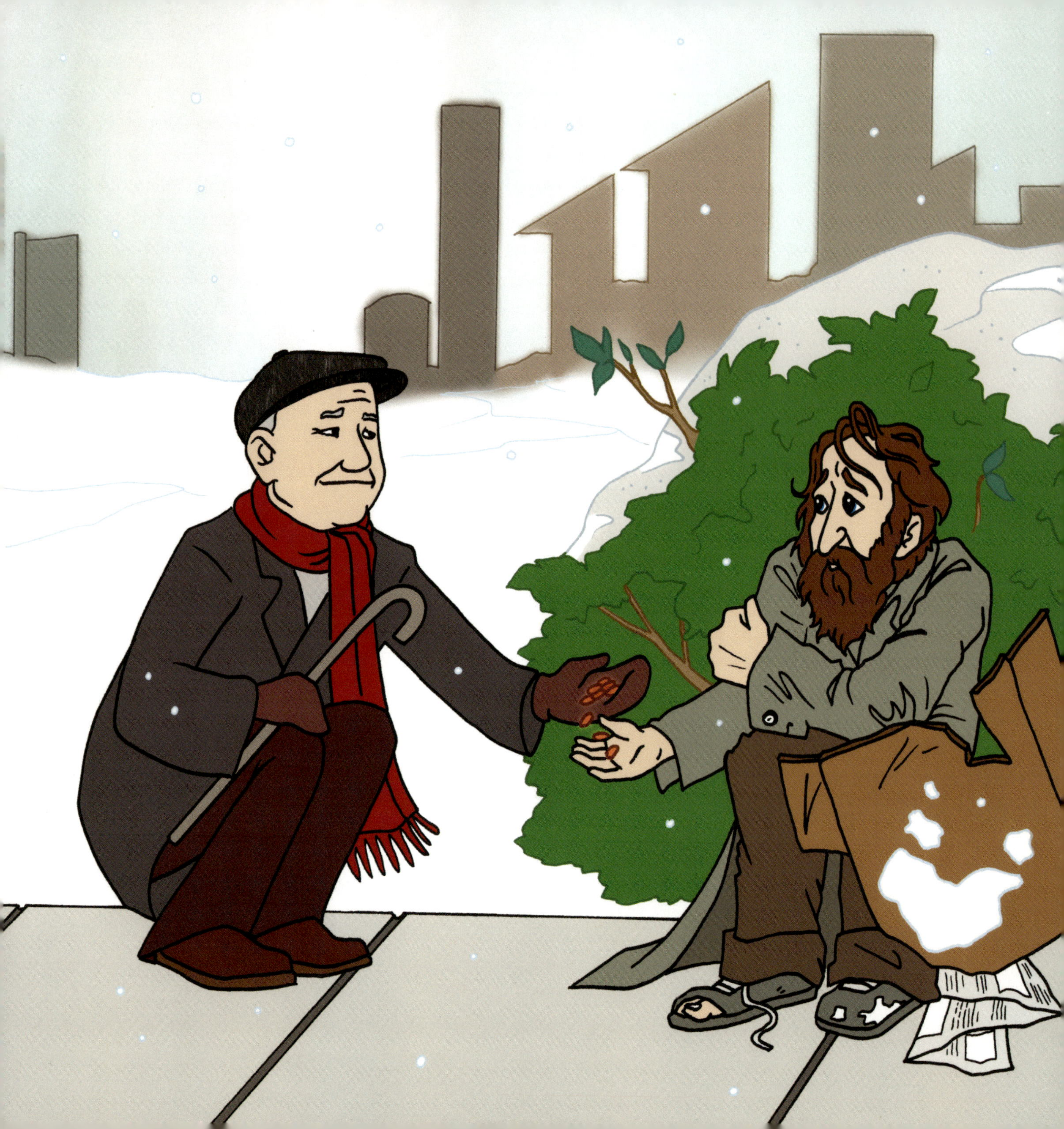

As he was walking, he came across a man who looked to be freezing. This man had no home and no family. He called the streets his home. The old man approached him as he was sitting outside his shelter and said, "Sir, Merry Christmas."

The man replied as his teeth chattered together, "Merry Christmas."

The old man looked at him and said, "I do not have much to give, but I do have this." He took all the pennies out of his pocket and handed them to the man. "Put one penny close to your heart, close your eyes, and make a wish. Maybe, just maybe, it will come true."

The man did as he requested and closed his eyes. "What did you wish for?" he said. "A hot cup of tea," said the homeless man.

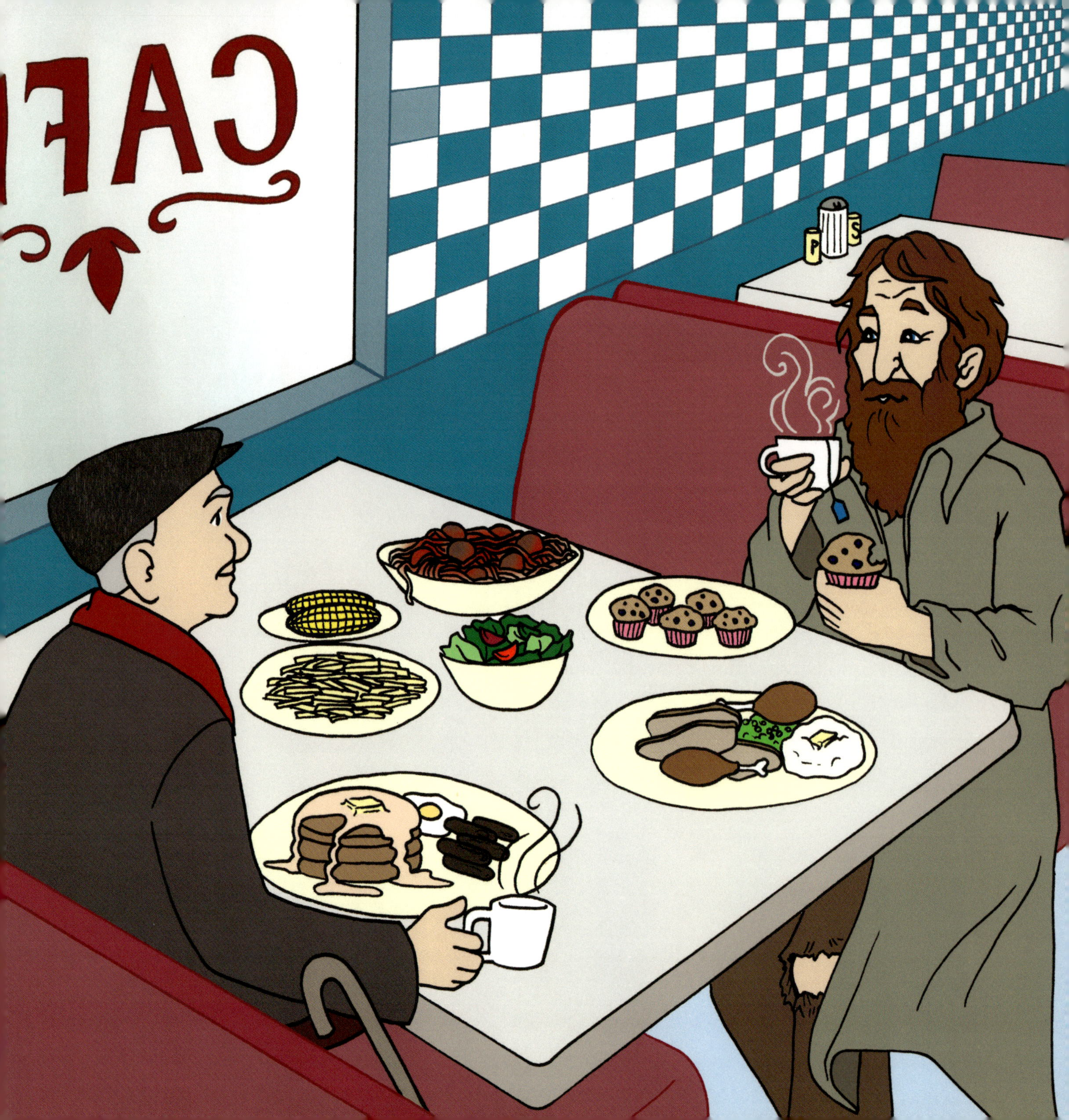

The older man chuckled and told the man to follow him. They both walked together in the snow until they came across a cafe, which was closed for the holidays. The old man reached into his pocket and took out a key and unlocked the door. You see, he owned this cafe. He told the homeless man to come whenever he needed for warmth from the cold or a nice, hot cup of tea. They drank their tea and ate the feast the man had prepared, and off the man went, with a "Thank you, Merry Christmas," and a smile on his face.

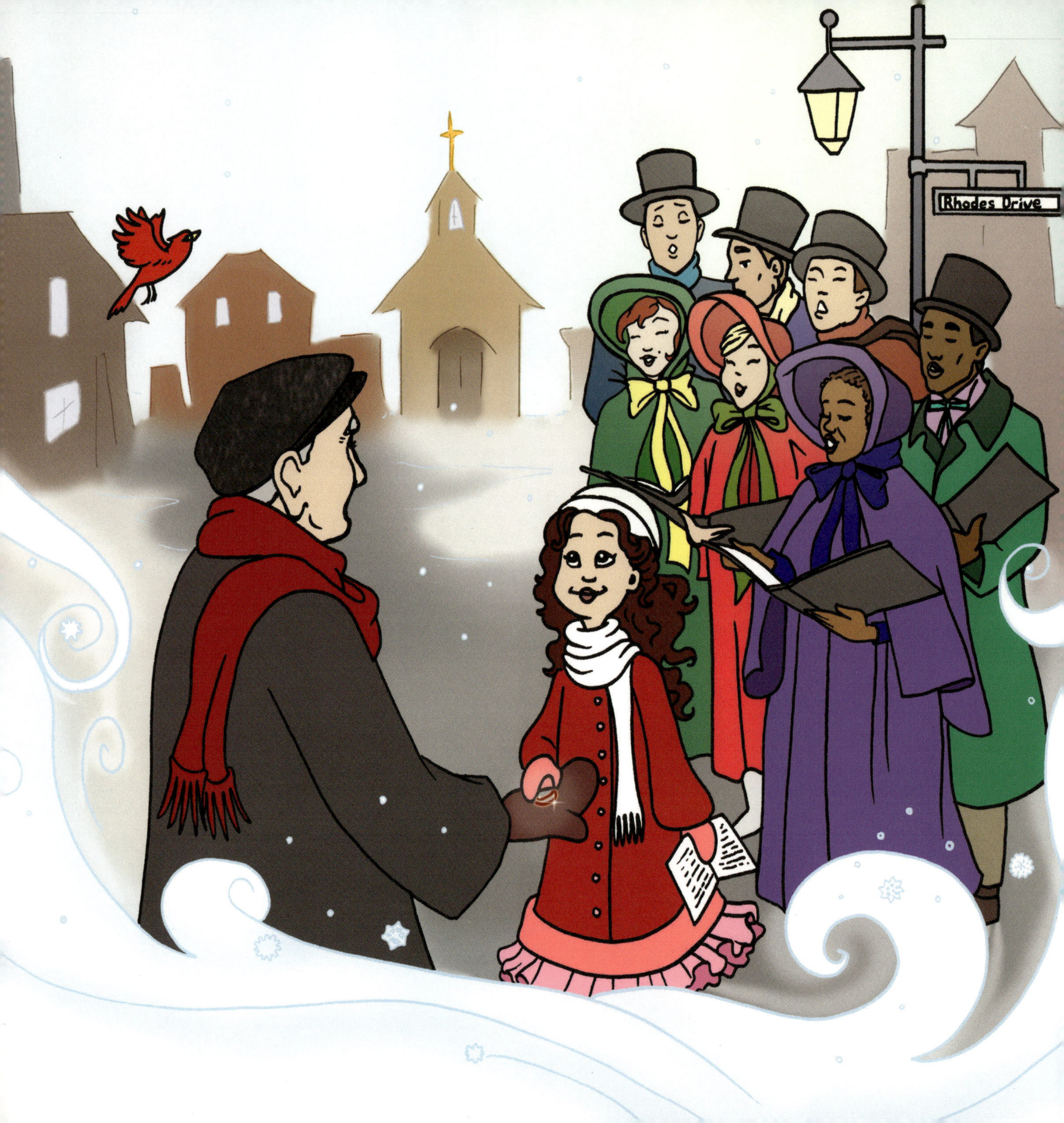
Rhodes Drive

As the night grew older and the snow became deeper, the old man realized that it was time to head home. While walking home he heard carolers singing on the nearby street corner. As he walked closer, he began to sing softly along with them. Among them he saw a cup sitting in the snow. He knew what it was for, so he reached into his pocket to put a penny in the cup, only to realize that he had no pennies left. A little girl came from the back of the singers and made her way to the front. She reached into her pocket and said, "Sir, I found this penny in the snow as we were walking here, and I picked it up. Normally, I would have walked by it, but something deep inside told me to pick it up and place it in my pocket. I don't know why, but after seeing you, I know now who I should give it to, and for some strange reason, I'm sure you will know what to do with it." The old man took the penny, placed it close to his heart, closed his eyes, and made a wish.

LaVergne, TN USA
09 November 2010
204112LV00002B